The Augustan Building Programme

Was Augustus trying to prove anything?

by Barry Vale

Contents

Abstract

This is an analysis of the Augustan building programme with reference to the motivations, aims, and achievements of Augustus during his long reign as Roman Emperor, which was effectively from 31 BC after the defeat of Mark Anthony, through to his death in 14 AD. Included in the discussions, aside from the direct influences and policies of the Augustan regime, will be the other political, social, economic and religious influences upon the Augustan building programme. The focus will be on the various objectives of the Augustan building programme such as the commemoration of events and the demonstration of political and military power, plus propaganda messages.

The influence of Roman culture and religious beliefs will be discussed, as well as signs of personal and Imperial prestige that emerged as a result of all the influences upon the programme. Therefore, the following will debate whether Augustus had any particular messages that the Augustan building programme was intended to convey, what these buildings were supposed to show people, or even the arguments that the buildings were supposed to prove to people. Augustus was not the first leader and certainly will not be the last leader to believe that building programmes could have an important role in the strength and prestige of his regime. By the time Augustus became Roman Emperor there were certainly messages that he would have liked to convey to his subjects, his personal rivals, and also towards countries or empires that rivalled, or potentially rivalled the Roman Empire during his reign.

Finally the following will analyse the messages that the Augustan building project conveyed to posterity, as well as to those people such as Seutonius, Virgil and Livy that were contemporaries of the Emperor Augustus. Augustus himself wrote of his achievements in the Rae Gestae towards the end of his long reign. It is also worth mentioning the reaction of contemporaries to the building programme as they saw the buildings in their full glory, and as they were the ones that the Augustan regime wanted to give messages to. The subsequent course of history meant that much of the Augustan building programme was destroyed. The remains are impressive enough so the effects when the buildings were newly completed must have been quite astounding. Motivations to be discussed include propaganda, commemoration, the support of traditional Roman religion, and the quest for power and prestige alongside pragmatic political, social, and economic reasons for the Augustan building programme. The discussion will be highly focused upon the influences that Augustus and his administration had on the planning and implementation of the building programme, as what Augustus wanted, he usually got. Given his own immense personal wealth and the healthier state of Roman finances, brought about by his administrations' efficiency, money was not an issue that prevented Augustus from carrying out his building programme.

The ways in which the Augustan building programme was the same and the ways it was different from traditional Roman architecture will be assessed. The influence that the Augustan building programme had upon future Roman buildings will also be discussed.

Introduction

The man known to his contemporaries and posterity as Augustus
Caesar began life as Gaius Julius Caesar Octavianus in 63 BC
although he was often referred to as Octavian. Julius Caesar
introduced him to public life whilst he was still a boy (Crystal, 1998,
p. 53). Augustus' father was a Roman senator who died whilst he
was a boy, although the family link that proved invaluable for his
future political and military career was through his mother Atia, she
was the niece of Julius Caesar. Circumstances turned Augustus from
a protégé and adopted son of Julius Caesar to a political and military
leader more powerful and formally more established than his mentor
had ever been. Like many Romans he was taught the importance of
family and traditional Roman values such as mental and physical
toughness, as well as a strong respect for legality. In many respects
these lessons were strong influences not only upon the Augustan
building programme, yet also upon his political and military
decision-making processes (Speake, 1994, p.93). Previously Julius
Caesar had gained wide-ranging military and political powers in
Rome as a pro-consul and 'dictator for life'. Julius Caesar's military
campaigns such as the invasion of Gaul meant he had been admired
and feared in almost equal measures, although the legions he
commanded were very loyal to him, leading Senators and other
generals were envious of his power. It was Brutus that killed Julius
Caesar in 44 BC to prevent him from becoming king and ending the
Roman Republic by reintroducing the monarchy (Boardman, Griffin,
& Murray, 1988, p. 121). Julius Caesar left all his wealth and
possessions to his only male relative, Augustus. Fortunately for
Augustus, the loyalty of Julius Caesar's battle hardened legions was
also passed on to him, an invaluable asset for the seizing of power in
the subsequent civil wars (Castleden, 2005, p. 96).

As his power grew, Augustus did not officially end the Roman
Republic as he chose not to do so (Ramage & Ramage, 1991, p. 79).
However as will be described, the old Republican institutions were
sidelined as Augustus centralised power into his own hands, gaining
the titles of 'imperator' and 'princeps', literally being known as
emperor and first citizen of Rome. Although imperator was only

originally a title given to a general or admiral that had won a battle, such a victory gave them the right to march through Rome, whilst many had built or renovated temples to commemorate their achievements. These titles demonstrate that Augustus successfully increased his public prestige, whilst even those with Republican scruples had to admit that Augustus brought peace, prosperity, and stability to Rome after decades of civil war and Republican decay (Roberts, 1996, p. 53). Augustus may have made frequent public protestations about just being an ordinary Roman citizen doing an extraordinary job, yet his occasional façade of modesty could not disguise his systematic accumulation of power, wealth, and public offices. The very adoption of the title Augustus Caesar itself was of great symbolic significance, it was a title that he had earned through the virtue of his political and military achievements. It was also a means of ensuring a greater degree of loyalty within the Roman Empire, especially from the army and the Senate (Goldsworthy, 2003 p. 236).

By changing his name from Octavian to Augustus Caesar he was demonstrating that he was greater than any other living person was; in fact he was almost divine. Augustus did not just change his name and his image; he also wanted to leave his mark upon Rome and its empire. The change of name was a decisive influence on the consolidation of power and the decision to expand the Augustan building programme to befit the image of a semi-divine saviour of his city and his country. Arguably, the concept behind and the completion of the Augustan building programme were part of Augustus' plans to improve, indeed transform Rome for the better. If the glory and splendour of Rome increased it would therefore increase the prestige and the glory of the man who ruled Rome. Building programmes had been used before in Rome and other places to demonstrate power and prestige so Augustus was not using a new concept (Holland, 2003 p. 366). Augustus during his long reign as Roman Emperor carried out a building programme in Rome and throughout the Roman Empire on a massive scale. This much is undisputed by both his contemporaries and historians (Boardman, Griffin, & Murray, 1988, p. 121). However, as the next three chapters will demonstrate the motivations behind the Augustan building programme have caused controversy and debate.

At this point it would also be useful to give a basic discussion of Roman art, architecture, and culture that existed at the time of Augustus. The Romans worshipped various Gods and deities, such as the sun god, Jupiter, Mars, Apollo, and Venus. Mars and Venus were generally favoured as legend linked them to the founding of Rome itself. Many Romans held a strong belief that their city was the greatest city upon earth as Mars and Venus had divinely inspired its founding. Before the onset of the Augustan building programme, the most well built buildings were frequently the many temples in Rome, whilst most other public buildings and private dwellings were made of brick (Beard & Crawford, 2004 p. 25). Religious beliefs and practices had traditionally played an important part in the haphazardly constructed architecture of Rome, although attention was often given to the appearance of temples, little thought was given to their exact locations as Rome was a city that had never used systematic urban planning (Platner, 1926). Those Romans that were financially able to do so had often built or reconstructed temples, as a sign of religious fervour, as well as being a way to gain prestige. Generals, Senators, and the wealthier aristocratic families had been the main patrons of temple construction and repair, although there were no precedents for the scale of construction and renovation carried out during the Augustan building programme. Due to Rome's vulnerability to flooding, the reconstruction of temples was a fairly frequent event. Before the onset of the Augustan building programme, Rome's temples had been greatly influenced by Greek designs and architecture (Davies, 1996, p.174). The political career of Augustus would however change the purposes of art and architecture in the Roman world. Art had generally been for enjoyment or the promotion of the patrons, whilst architecture usually served practical roles. The Augustan building programme would prove to be the first time that the ruling Roman regime used art to serve an overtly political agenda (Ramage & Ramage, 1991 p. 79).

Roman architecture had usually made pillars or columns merely decorative, instead the Romans had tended to emphasis arches, vaults, or domes. The concentration on rounded architectural forms was the main way, in which the Roman building designs differed from the earlier Greek building designs they were outwardly based upon. To improve upon the strength and durability of Roman buildings these buildings were built in brick and concrete, with the more prestigious projects then being clad in marble. Such construction techniques reduced the building times, and also gave the advantages of reducing the amount of marble needed, as well as allowing for the inclusion of domes or other features in the final designs. Architects and stone masons that were used to design the buildings employed such construction techniques for the completed Augustan building programme (Neal, 2004, p.12). Apart from the more obvious Greek influence there was also a discernible Etruscan influence on Roman architecture, although the Augustan building programme was proof that the Romans had developed a separate style from those influences (Speake, 1994, p.60). Roman architecture was not all about designing buildings to look beautiful it was about projecting an image of power, yet also an expression of universal cultural, political, and social values (Wheeler, 1964, p.23). The Augustan building programme was able to take advantage of improvements in the design and production of concrete domes and higher quality kiln-fired bricks. Such techniques were harnessed to transform Rome Ironically the finest examples of these being used in new buildings during the Augustan period was in Turin, for instance the Porta Palantina (Boardman, Griffin, & Murray, 1988, p. 367). The Augustan building programme spread from Rome to other parts of Italy, France, Germany, and Spain, notable sites include the Temple of Mercury at Baiae (Boardman, Griffin, & Murray, 1988, p. 367).

There was another less glamorous side to the Augustan building programme that received less attention from contemporaries, the building of new roads. The need for road building and repairing had an influence upon the Augustan building programme, as the Augustan regime was pragmatic to believe that economic growth and the construction of substantial growth were restricted by poor road links. Roads and bridges may have offered less chance for showing off or commemorating people or events. Nonetheless, the construction of roads and bridges was vitally important for the political, economic and military effectiveness of Rome and its empire. The construction of roads was nothing new, and Roman roads were amongst the best in the Ancient World. Augustus organised the building of new roads to improve lines of communication and supply within Rome itself and with the Roman Empire. Roads carried more food into the city and also allowed Roman legions to reach trouble spots more effectively. The roads and bridges built as a complement to the Augustan building programme had a long life span. Some of the Augustan bridges are still in use, in Rome and in cities such as Rimini (Parry, 2005, p.74). Augustus made good use of a road-based postal service that allowed relatively rapid communications across his dominions. Maps and road guides were available not only for Rome but also for the provinces such as Gaul and Spain (Parry, 2005, pp.92-94).

Chapter 1 Obtaining Power To Gain Glory

The way in which Julius Caesar had died was to influence the form and the direction of the Augustan building programme. Explanations for Augustus initially commencing the Augustan building programme for the purpose of commemoration have been plausibly argued. The concept of erecting buildings to commemorate events such as military victories, or the achievements and lives of powerful people that had died was not completely novel when Augustus took power. However, some of the events, people, and the ways in which they were commemorated were different in respect of the Augustan building programme. Previously victorious roman generals had built monuments to mark their victories, and their successful conquests. Roman generals had the right to hold victory parades on the streets of Rome, they could sell prisoners into slavery, and use the booty from their victories to fund building projects or lavish lifestyles. Roman leaders, prior to Augustus, had traditionally built or funded the building of religious temples, sports arenas, and other public buildings. The temples chosen for building or renovation would often be those of the God or Gods victorious generals believed were upon their side. Julius Caesar had been keen on building sports arenas, funding games, and subsidising bread to gain public support against the Senate and his rivals (Liberati & Bourbon, 2004, p.42). There were of course mixed objectives and influences for such building projects, a concern for ordinary Romans (whether citizens or not), that can be summed up as the search for prestige and power. There was also the desire to gain votes in tribunal elections and to gain influence over the Senate, either for themselves or their supporters. A politician as astute as Augustus was certainly aware that the Augustan building programme would contribute to the achievement of his political, social, and cultural objectives (Claridge, 1998). Augustus could and did point out that part of the Augustan building programme had the objective of fulfilling Julius Caesar's plans to greatly increase the grandness of Rome. Julius Caesar's assassination had put such extensive renovation and regeneration plans on hold until the ensuing civil war was brought to an end. Caesar's plans had included proposals for a new Senate House, new public theatres, and public libraries

(Rodgers, 2005, p.21).

The fact that Julius Caesar had planned a major building programme of his own for Rome meant that Augustus could publicly state that the Augustan building programme was indeed the continuation of previous plans and was therefore a means of commemorating Julius Caesar's political and military achievements. Augustus could portray himself as the man that finished the political, military, and architectural projects or policies that Julius Caesar had started. Linking the Augustan building programme to the memory of Caesar was certainly a sound political move on Augustus' part, for he owed the opportunity to gain control of Rome to the patronage that Caesar had given him (Zanker, 1988). On a broader political, military, and social level, Julius Caesar had been popular with ordinary Romans, large sections of the Roman army, as well as being deified as a God after his murder. Treating Julius Caesar as a God meant that Augustus could commemorate him by building new temples and amending existing temples, most notably the Mars Ultor (Rodgers, 2005, p.21). Commemoration also included completing the other public buildings planned such as the theatre of Marcellus. The theatre of Marcellus featured seats set in raised concrete bases framed by marble clad engaged columns that formed an impressive series of arcades (Boardman, Griffin, & Murray, 1988, p. 365).

There had been pragmatic reasons why Julius Caesar had wanted to complete a substantial building programme for Rome itself. The struggle for power and renewed civil wars after Caesar's death had only increased the urgency for instigating a pragmatic building programme to make Rome a better city to govern, control, and for the better off at least to live in. After decades of intermittent civil wars Rome was in many respects in a sad state and needed an extensive building programme to reduce its problems (Garnsey & Saller, 1987 p. 8). However, it was not just civil wars that had taken their toils upon Rome. The population of Rome had expanded to around one million inhabitants, by far the largest city in the world at that point. As a consequence housing conditions, especially for the poorer classes were overcrowded and basic. Rome had outmoded transport facilities and was also prone to food shortages and flooding. Julius Caesar had hoped that his building programme would rectify these problems. Rome's problems did not help social stability or economic growth; the city had been a victim of its own chaotic growth. Implementing the reconstruction of Rome was certainly a fitting commemoration to Julius Caesar (le Glay, Voison & le Bohec, 2005, p.168). Augustus was not able to implement the Augustan building programme until he had complete control of Rome and its empire. It took thirteen years of hard fighting before Augustus defeated Mark Anthony in 31 BC (Boardman, Griffin & Murray, 1988, p.124). Once he gained complete control of Rome, Augustus used military campaigns as well as the Augustan building programme to increase his prestige. The borders of the Roman Empire were extended from the Rhine to the Danube, although the Germanic tribes strongly resisted further expansion (Garnsey & Saller, 1987, p.7). The first step of the Augustan building programme was reforming its administration, introducing rudimentary urban planning and dividing the city into 14 regions (Platner, 1926).

Julius Caesar and Mark Anthony gave Augustus an insight into how the consolidation of political and military power was not always easy to achieve. For instance, although Julius Caesar had been a very capable military commander, and a charismatic political leader, his public relations or propaganda skills could have been better. Once he was made dictator for life Julius Caesar seemed also to believe that his personal safety was no longer threatened. However Julius Caesar, as previously noted had been very popular with the majority of the Roman army and also many ordinary Romans (Boardman, Griffin, & Murray, 1988, p. 121). For Julius Caesar putting on games, arranging grain supplies, besides finding land and money for his legions were logical means of consolidating his power within Rome. Not everybody had wanted Julius Caesar to successfully consolidate his position as dictator (Liberati & Bourbon, 2004, p.42). His popularity did not extend to a large minority of Roman Senators and parts of the aristocracy, many of whom feared his political intentions were towards overthrowing the Roman Republic, and his links with the plebeian elements of Roman society. Caesar publicly denied that he wished to become the king of Rome. Brutus and Cassius claimed that they had plotted the death of Caesar to protect both the institutions of the Roman Republic and the political, social, and economic privileges of the Roman aristocracy (Boardman, Griffin, & Murray, 1988, p.121). The key for success to Augustus was to keep the loyalty of those that had supported Julius Caesar on board, whilst trying to obtain support from Republican factions (Holland, 2003, p.370).

The fate of Julius Caesar provided Augustus with the political lesson that publicly ending the very existence of the Roman Republic, or even the appearance of subverting its institutions could drastically increase the chances of provoking widespread opposition to the existence and continuance of the Augustan regime. Such a move could even have proved to be fatal. It is not surprising that Augustus would claim to be continuing the Republican regime, rather than ending it. He also took steps to ensure his personal safety, for instance forming the Praetorian Guards (Roberts, 1996, p.53). Unlike many of his successors, Augustus died of old age rather than being murdered or killed in battle, he consolidated his position so well that nobody proved capable of removing him (le Glay, Voison, le Boehec, 2005, p.168).

On the other hand Mark Anthony's biggest mistakes had been to appear to be unpatriotic and immoral. Committing adultery was not usually condemned amongst the Roman elites, although leaving wives and children to live with somebody else could cause gossip. Mark Anthony had left his second wife, who just happened to be Augustus' sister for the enchanting Queen Cleopatra of Egypt. That marriage had been part of the political deal between Augustus and Mark Anthony, and it was a sign of their (not very strong) personal friendship and political alliance. Alienating Augustus was certainly not the shrewdest move that Mark Anthony ever made (le Glay, Voison, le Boehec, 2005, p.168). The two men had split the Roman Empire between themselves, Mark Anthony seemed determined to establish his own empire based upon Egypt, to be passed on to his children by Cleopatra. Mark Anthony inadvertently allowed Augustus the opportunity to rally public opinion in Rome and the Western Provinces behind his cause to become sole ruler of the Roman Empire. It was sensible strategy on Augustus' part to publicly state it was a war against Cleopatra, rather than a continuation of civil war (le Glay, Voison, le Boehec, 2005, p.168). To defeat Mark Anthony the Senate gave Augustus extraordinary powers; there were also public oaths of allegiance to Augustus in 32 BC. All the events leading up to the final defeat of Mark Anthony demonstrated that Augustus was a master of public relations and propaganda. Caesar of course had enjoyed similar extraordinary powers, yet had not lived long enough to use those powers to their full extent. The way in which the Augustan building programme was completed arguably served useful public relations and propaganda purposes for Augustus (Zanker, 1988). The capture of Egypt had another effect on the Romans, for a while it was fashionable to have Egyptian style paintings and ornamental objects like sphinxes and other cult objects (Boardman, Griffin, & Murray, 1988, p. 371).

However, it did not take Augustus too long to construct a temple in Caesar's honour after Mark Anthony had been defeated. By 29 BC the temple of the Divine Julius was erected and specifically honoured Julius Caesar, although the victories of Augustus especially that of Actium were also commemorated. Augustus noticed that such building projects were ideal opportunities for commemorating his achievements at the same time as remembering Caesar. The new Senate House, renamed the Curia Julius was finally completed. Augustus wanted the Senate to realise that he, just like Caesar held the real power in Rome. Although Augustus intended to by pass the Senate, he did not publicly want to overthrow the institutions of the Roman Republic. Naming the Senate House after Caesar was not only to commemorate him, it was symbolic of where power resided in Rome (le Glay, Voisin, & le Bohec, 2005, p.185). Caesar had also started the construction of new law courts in Rome, which was interrupted by the civil wars that followed his death. Again Augustus had the building completed and it became known as the Basilica Julia. The courts commemorated Caesar as well as serving the practical purpose of dispensing justice in Rome (Boardman, Griffin & Murray, 1988, p.171). Augustus was different from other Roman leaders in that he held more power than all his predecessors did, yet did not overtly show that power off by closing the Senate (Seutonius, p.99).

The undoubted centrepiece of the Augustan building programme was the Forum of Augustus, the main feature of which was the Mars Ultor; a temple dedicated to Mars, the God of War. Mars Ultor literally translates as 'Mars the Avenger'. Augustus intended that the Mars Ultor be used to commemorate Roman victories, such as Tiberius' victory against the Parthians in 20 BC (Goldsworthy, 2003, p.273). Augustus had promised to construct Mars Ultor, which he did once his grip on power was secure. The Mars Ultor was dedicated to Mars as Mars was the main god of Rome, Mars had brought Rome greatness so it was only right for Romans to honour Mars. Augustus was hoping that honouring Mars would bring himself and Rome even more greatness (Liberati & Bourbon, 2004, p36). Mars Ultor was a massive building that showed Augustus' intentions to show off his own power, wealth, and greatness. The temple of Mars Ultor also marked the successes of Rome's past, especially those of Julius Caesar who had originally planned to build the temple (Rodgers, 2005, p.21). The sheer scale of the Mars Ultor impressed contemporaries such as Ovid, just has it had been intended to do. Given Augustus' military background, and his reliance upon the military to keep his regime secure it is not surprising that the largest temple in the Augustan building programme was the Mars Ultor. To quote Ovid 'Huge the God and huge the temple' (Ovid, Fasti 5.551-3).

Mars Ultor included statues not only of Mars and Venus, yet also of Julius Caesar. At that point it did not feature any statues of Augustus inside the actual temple, as he was not deified until after his death. Other statues inside the temple included two of the most important men in Rome's development and expansion, Romulus and Aeneas. Romulus had founded the city of Rome and been its first king. Both men were claimed to be ancestors of Julius Caesar and Augustus. The defeat of Mark Anthony was commemorated using the bows of ships that fought at Actium and Augustus' subsequent conquest of Egypt. That was also a celebration of Augustus' victory. Outside the entrance to Mars Ultor was a statue of a four-horse chariot built at the request of the Senate as a means of honouring Augustus. In terms of architectural influences the Forum of

Augustus and the Mars Ultor were similar to, and inspired by the Forum of Julius Caesar and its centrepiece of the Temple to Venus; Genetrix. The similarity of design was deliberate as Augustus wished to be linked with Julius Caesar in people's thoughts. In religious and mythical terms it also made sense to put the temples dedicated to Mars and Venus together, as they had been lovers. Augustus again was using subtle links to increase his prestige, as it was believed that both he and Julius Caesar were descended from Mars and Venus (Ramage & Ramage, 1991, p. 83). Mars Ultor or other prestigious projects within the Augustan building programme had not impressed everybody. For instance the architect Vitruvius disapproved of the over extensive use of marble cladding as it was reducing the importance of more traditional building materials such as mud bricks. Vitruvius felt so strongly about the harmful affect of the Augustan building programme that he wrote ten volumes in defence of the virtues of Republican architecture (Boardman, Griffin, & Murray, 1988, p. 365).

Another major temple he had rebuilt to an impressive new standard as part of the Augustan building programme was that of Apollo Sosiarius. Another 82 temples were repaired using the considerable treasure seized from Mark Anthony and Cleopatra in Egypt. Augustus therefore, was keen about promoting traditional religion in Rome, as he believed that religion had helped to make Rome great and that greatness would increase if all Romans kept to their traditional religions (le Glay, Voison, le Boehec, 2005, p.168). The defeat of Mark Anthony allowed Augustus to reduce the size of the army by more than half, from 60 legions to 28 legions, with auxiliaries stationed in the provinces. The confiscated treasure from Egypt allowed him to settle veteran soldiers on their own lands, and therefore ensure that they were not a source of discontent. The reduction of the Roman army had indirect influences upon the Augustan building programme. Peace freed up resources to be spent on the building projects, whilst the victories that ended the conflicts were a theme of those building projects included in the Augustan building programme (Grant, 1996, p.12). The Forum of Augustus was not just built for the benefit of the worshippers of Mars the Avenger, or for the commemoration of Julius Caesar. The Forum was one of several venues across the city for gladiator fights and athletic contests (Seutonius p. 43). Augustus himself seems to have liked such games as forms of entertainment, and as a means of keeping ordinary Romans content, as well giving some of them jobs. Augustus manipulated sports festivals and games for propaganda purposes as astutely as he used the building programme, most notably in the form of the Secular Games of 17BC (le Glay, Voison, le Boehec, 2005, p.216).

There was another influence upon the Augustan building programme. Whilst Augustus was very keen about renovating and improving the architecture of Rome he did not seek to destroy the most historic buildings within the city. He certainly did not want anyone else outside of his regime pulling down buildings without official consent. For him there seemed to be little point in trying to improve the appearance of the city if people undermined the benefits of the Augustan building programme by ruining existing buildings. Measures to prevent building demolitions were linked with the introduction of urban planning. Augustus had a concern therefore, to ensure the preservation of monuments and old buildings to maintain Rome's rich cultural and architectural heritage. His concerns for the preservation of monuments and buildings were recorded upon bronze tablets at Herculaneum. Augustus was against 'the ruination of houses and towns, gives in peacetime the appearance of war.' People that deliberately damaged buildings could be fined and may even have to answer to the Senate for their actions (Schnapp, 1993, p.334).

Chapter 2 The Motives Of Augustus

Augustus' motivations and objectives for the Augustan building programme went beyond the need for commemoration of people and events that were linked to his regime. There were political, social, and economic motivations behind the concept and carrying out of the Augustan building programme. When added together these various motivations formed one overwhelming objective, the consolidation of Augustus' political and military power with its related reduction in power of the Senate and other institutional bodies of the Roman Republic. Augustus had known his regime was not secure until he held complete control of the army and had eliminated his main opponents (Claridge, 1998). The quest to consolidate the Augustan regime was undertaken, whilst Rome had witnessed the failure of capable men such as Julius Caesar and Mark Anthony to gain and consolidate their hold on power. Augustus did have strong advantages when it came for him to consolidate his power, advantages that included his great personal wealth, his family connections, and the loyalty of some of Rome's finest legions. As useful and wide-ranging as these advantages were, they did not guarantee that Augustus could consolidate and maintain his grip upon power in Rome and throughout the Roman Empire. For Augustus, as with any other ruler in the Ancient World, the consolidation of power relied upon a mixture of pragmatic measures, and what in modern terms would be described as public relations, spin, or propaganda. The constructions that made up the Augustan building programme certainly mixed up being pragmatic, public relations for the Augustan regime as well as showing off the status and prestige of Augustus himself (le Glay, Voisin, & le Bohec, 2005, p.185).

Augustus was careful to convey the image that he was the last available protector of the Roman Republic, as well as being the protector of the city itself. Augustus was careful to ensure that the new Senate House and the Curia Julius was finally completed. He could have left the Senate in its old building or closed it completely (although they occasionally sat at other sites). Nobody doubted that he could have abolished the Senate if he had wanted, after all over

300 Senators had been purged, imprisoned, or executed during the conflict against Brutus and Cassius. A further 2,000 members of the aristocracy and the gentry were sentenced to death, with thousands of farmers across Italy also evicted from their farms (Beard & Crawford, 2004, p.86). However, the closing of the Senate would have totally disproved his claims that he was only interested in preserving the Roman Republic instead of personal glory. After all improving Rome would bring him glory and prestige anyway. The Augustan regime's spin was that none of the buildings that were included in the Augustan building programme could have been used in the process of dismantling the Roman Republic. Instead Augustus argued that the construction of new law courts, temples, and sports arenas when combined with the renovation of Rome's old temples, demonstrated his tangible commitment to improving the infrastructure of the Roman Republic. In reality under the rule of Augustus, Rome had become 'a military autocracy disguised as a revitalised Republic' (Kemp, 2000, p. 40). However it was an autocracy in which people were free to live the Roman dream, of a quiet and peaceful life that allowed the hope of leaving the city for a comfortable villa in the countryside (Horace, Epodes, 2.1-6).

From a public relations perspective the Augustan building programme was literally the concrete (or frequently the marble clad) proof that the glory of Rome had been restored and indeed increased (Galinsky, 1996). The buildings of the Augustan Building Programme could be partially constructed of marble due to the new sources of it that were found and quarried in north-west Italy, which allowed Augustus to replace many of the brick public buildings during his long reign (Honour & Fleming, 1999, p.202). In order to promote social harmony and reduce the potential for public disorder. Thus Augustus repaired and increased public facilities to improve the quality of life for many Romans, he may have been motivated by the wish to create social harmony and political stability yet he seemed to also want to improve peoples standard of live (Ramage & Ramage, 1991 p. 117). The desire to clean up the city in a literal as well a metaphorical sense was an influence upon the Augustan building programme. The new buildings not only made Rome look better their construction prompted clean ups in the surrounding areas (le Glay, Voisin, & le Bohec, 2005, p. 68).

The regime's extensive building programme was a potent symbol that the Roman Republic was revitalised, and that Augustus' wise administration was making Rome a better place to live in. The determination to improve the look of Rome was a strong driving force or influence upon the Augustan building programme. The Curia Julius, the Forum of Augustus with the magnificent Mars Ultor as its focal point were a reflection of Rome's greatness, indeed they had only been built due to the prosperity, peace, and stability that Augustus had brought to Rome. The regime also had the willingness to spend its revenue on the building programme (Galinsky, 1996). The buildings that were part of the Augustan building programme were designed to be bigger, better, and grander than previous buildings as a direct result of Rome having greater stability than before, in other words the Augustan building programme was a dividend of peace. The Augustan building programme was inaugurated to rebuild Rome, not only because parts of the city need renovating, but also as he could do so with the considerable resources that he had available to him (Galinksy, 1996).

Augustus was rebuilding Rome not only because parts of it needed renovating, but also because he could do so. The Augustan building programme could have been used to show the virtues of the Roman republic, which had been unable to provide peace and stability as the greed and ambitions of generals and Senators had grown out of control. Instead, the Augustan building programme was used to show that Augustus had saved Rome from civil war and decadence with the intention of making her more powerful than ever before and restoring moral, cultural, and social values (Favro, 1996). The message that Augustus wanted the Augustan building programme to convey was that he alone was responsible for restoring the greatness of Rome. He had done so by putting an end to moral, religious, and political decadence and containing the ambitions of Senators and generals that did nothing but harm the peace, prosperity, and stability of Rome. The Augustan building programme was able to have such big breathtaking and imposing buildings due to newly restored peace and stability, which meant that Rome's money could be spent on such projects, rather than being spent on wars. Augustus contended that he had brought back peace and stability for the benefit of Rome and everybody within the Roman Empire, his actions had also saved the Roman Republic (Holland, 2003, p.372).

Augustus was reluctant to admit via the Augustan building programme or any other means of communication that he had restored peace and stability at the cost of the de facto; the termination of the Roman Republic. The Augustan building programme was a commemoration of Rome's past, a celebration of its present as well as a projection of its future. Taken at face value the Augustan building programme and the proclamations of Augustus himself, people may have believed that the Roman Republic would not only survive it would prosper (Holland, 2003, p. 371). In reality many people expected what Augustus had wanted, the future for Rome was an Imperial one rather than a republican future. The aim of establishing a secure Imperial dynasty influenced Augustus' political policies, as well as having an influence upon the Augustan building programme. For instance, the Mars Ultor and the Arca Pacis Augustae had depictions of Augustus' actual blood and adopted relatives (Ramage & Ramage, 1991, p. 79).

Although the institutions of the Roman Republic were intact, they became increasingly irrelevant. Augustus certainly planned for a dynasty of princeps to continue ruling Rome after his death. The urge to present the grandness of the new Rome was a strong influence upon the building programme. Passing on his position to a successor was the ultimate proof that his plans and achievements would continue after his death. The Augustan building programme may have been the magnificent symbols of Rome's success under Augustus, yet without successors to consolidate his work the Augustan building programme would have just been a series of expensive white elephants. The search for an able successor turned out to be harder and more complex than Augustus had originally anticipated. Augustus only had one child of his own, a daughter Julia who could not inherit any of his offices. He adopted Tiberius at an early stage of his reign. Although he advised Tiberius he did not regard him as a natural successor. Other potential heirs were groomed, yet either proved unsatisfactory or Augustus simply outlived them. Agrippa could have been a strong contender to become the next princeps and he was involved in projects related to the Augustan building programme. At first Augustus considered Agrippa to be an invaluable asset to the effectiveness of the Augustus regime. Agrippa put simply, was a man that got the job done, which was why he was entrusted with overseeing the construction of some of the projects of the Augustan building programme. If Augustus did have doubts that Agrippa may have been attempting to grab some of the prestige gained by the Augustan building programme for himself, he did not show it publicly. He did not however, remove Agrippa from any offices before the latter's premature death. All the public acclaim for the Augustan building programme belonged to Augustus. In fact, on the numerous occasions that Augustus left Rome it was Agrippa that was left in charge of the city (Grant, 1996, p.11).

Roman architecture especially its temples, were heavily influenced by the buildings of Greece. The buildings of the Augustan building programme continued the Roman tendency to have their buildings functional and practical, ahead of their overall design feature. The Pantheon completed in 27 BC under the guidance of Agrippa, featured a magnificent dome in its roof that was wider than later buildings such as the basilica of St Peter's. The dome was supposed to be the most prominent part of the building, intended to fill it with light and to turn people's attention towards the sky. The dome if you like was a link between the earth and the heavens were the Gods could be found. The extra level of light allowed into the building by the dome could allow worshippers to believe that the sun god was there with them. The Pantheon was therefore a fine example of Roman architecture and was an example of highly advanced architecture not to mention engineering. Unlike other examples of the Augustan Building Programme it has survived, although it was heavily modified to become a church, that of Santa Maria Rotunda ad Martyres (Davies, 1996, p.174). The Pantheon was an extraordinary architectural achievement; it was a temple that abandoned the more traditional Greek influenced temple designs. Indeed the central attraction of the Pantheon was its dome, rather than the many fine statues of the various deities who were worshipped upon the site. Nobody could have blamed Agrippa if he had wanted to take the merit for the completion of the Pantheon (Honour & Fleming, 1999, p.202).

When Augustus' daughter first husband died it was Agrippa who was chosen to be her next husband. Agrippa and Julia had three sons; one of whom Augustus had hoped would succeed him. As fate turned out two of his grandsons died before Augustus, whilst the youngest grandson was considered mentally unfit for office. Agrippa was always Augustus' closest friend and political ally and was therefore greatly missed after his death in 12 BC. The death of Agrippa coupled with the deaths or unsuitability of Agrippa's sons meant that Augustus eventually accepted Tiberius as his successor. Augustus wanted to bequeath all of his offices and power to a family member out of a strong sense of family. The sense of family was strong in Rome, especially amongst the aristocracy and wealthier classes. There was the factor that leaving the succession to a relative would allow the stability of Rome to continue, especially as the army might not be loyal to somebody who was not related to Augustus (Grant, 1996, p.12).

There was a feature of the Augustan building programme, which carried on a traditional Roman practice. The artists, architects, stone masons, and sculptors that actually did the construction work on the building programme remained nameless and unknown to all but Augustus or the civil servants that hired them. The tradition of anonymity explains why all the artistic and architectural achievements of Rome were always associated with the names of the patrons that commissioned such projects and ultimately paid for them. For Augustus it did not matter who designed or built the temples, theatres, forums, and sports arenas that formed the Augustan building programme, they were just nameless workers that did their jobs very well and then got on with the next project. This traditional approach to building programmes meant all the prestige that came from the Augustan building programme went to Augustus and nobody else. Perhaps it would have been dangerous for anybody else to take the credit as Augustus would have taken such a move as an insult at best and an attempt to take his power from him at worst (Wheeler, 1964, p.9).

Chapter 3 Building To Put Propaganda In Place

The Augustan building programme was an essential part of the Augustus regime's propaganda and publicity objectives. Parts of the regime's propaganda remained constant throughout its existence, whilst other aspects of propaganda were adopted to suit particular circumstances. At the start of the regime Augustus' grip on power was not secure, aside from his loyal supporters, many Romans were unsure of him and his motives. Rome had endured years of civil wars and anarchy, whilst Augustus had been a prominent figure in those events. Critics and cynics could have been forgiven for believing that the new regime would be short lived and that Augustus was just another general that wished to be a dictator who would put his greed for wealth and power ahead of Rome. Not many expected a long period of stability; they expected a short brutal dictatorship or continued chaotic decline. The Augustus regime wanted to use propaganda to publicly declare that Augustus' rule was strong, stable and exactly what Rome needed to recover from civil war and Republican decay. The Augustan building programme fitted into the regime's propaganda strategy in various ways. The overall aim of the various propaganda messages linked with the Augustan building programme was that Augustus was the last man to be able to restore Rome to its former glory and then to make its future even greater.

The projects that were part of the Augustan building programme to fit in with the regime's publicity strategy were built on a larger scale to be more impressive, to convey the message that all Romans should be confident of present and future greatness. New imposing buildings would not be built on such a scale if the regimes that built them were weak and insecure. Not only did the regime rely on the Augustan building programme to project the public image that it was strong, successful and competent, it used poets, writers, and theatres to convey the same message. There was a high rate of literacy in Rome, which meant that all but the poorest sections of Roman society could be influenced by written material. Augustus was well aware that the vast majority of Romans believed that Rome was destined for greatness and that there was a well-developed understanding of Roman traditions and history. The buildings constructed as part of the Augustan building programme had inscriptions on them to convey the regime's messages for the literate, as well as statues and names chosen to convey such messages to those that were illiterate. The regime cultivated links with writers and artists to recruit their services to convey its messages. Augustus was a generous patron of the arts; the construction of the Augustan building programme and the production of pro-regime propaganda provided plenty of opportunities for many artists and writers (Zanker, 1988). The Augustan period became widely regarded as a golden age for Roman arts and literature. Therefore, the Augustus regime was very successful in conveying the message that it was restoring Roman culture and traditions through greater patronage and the Augustan building programme. The stability that the Augustus regime achieved made all of that possible. In the Aeneid, Virgil emphasises the need for strong yet fair rule that improves everything for everybody, a fitting description for the aims of Augustus.

'Make it your task, Roman, to rule the peoples by your command; to impose the habit of peace, to spare those who submit, and to conquer the proud' (Virgil, vi 851- 3).

Aside from literal giants such as Virgil, Livy and Seutonius singing the regime's praises, Augustus himself was an accomplished writer, most notably the Res Gestae which was a potent justification of all his policies and action, including the completion of the Augustan building programme. In the Res Gestae, Augustus proclaimed that he had 'built the Curia, and the Chalcidicum next to it, the temple of Apollo on the Palantine with its porticoes, the temple of the Divine Iuliuis, the Lupercal, the portico at the Flaminian Circus (Augustus, Res Gestae, 19).

Besides emphasising the cultural and artistic merits of the Augustus regime, the Augustan building programme and other forms of publicity defended the political merits and foundations of the regime. For pragmatic political reasons the Augustus regime based it legitimacy and creditability on the concept that was the continuance of the Roman Republic (Kemp, 2000, p. 40). As already discussed in the previous chapters, such a shrewd propaganda strategy originated from Augustus' own political astuteness. The regime derived it powers from other various offices that Augustus either held himself or manipulated himself to expect the maximum level of influence. Whilst being made a king would have offered him more formal and legal powers, this would have provoked vehement and violent condemnations that would have threatened the security of its head. Augustus intended that the Augustan building programme should therefore convey the message that he was continuing the Roman Republic and not usurping it for the selfish exercise of power. Augustus authorised the construction of the Augustan building programme through his various political, religious, secular and military positions. At various points during the Augustus regime he was consul, head of the tribunes and the highest priest of Rome's state religion. The Augustan building programme was intended to reconstruct the economic, legal, transport and religious infrastructures of Rome in order to reverse the decadence of the Roman Republic. Officially the message conveyed was that the Augustan regime was making the Roman Republic vibrant and stronger than ever. This message was clearly and precisely conveyed on numerous occasions. Such a message was not strictly true and was only believed by those who wanted to believe it to be true. The messages that were conveyed by the Augustan building programme contributed to the development of Imperial cults that were not put to an end until the adoption of Christianity as the state religion (Zanker, 1998).

In practical terms, although the Augustan regime had maintained the institutions of the Roman Republic and the Augustan building programme had repaired and expanded the infrastructures that could be visibly linked to the Republican institutions, political and constitutional power had been shifted to Augustus and his successors (Galinsky, 1996, p.79). Augustus and his regime did not deny that he held extraordinary powers, yet claimed that such powers were needed to prevent a return to anarchy and civil wars that prevailed before his defeat of Mark Anthony (Kemp, 2000, p. 40). These concepts kept the majority of Romans content, Augustus holding wider powers in return for giving Rome at peace was a fair exchange. He also managed to keep the army, the tribunes, and the majority of the aristocracy and the Senate loyal to him. Not everybody was fooled by the regime's stance that it was preserving the Roman Republic. Staunch Republicans within the aristocracy and the Senate did not believe the regime's propaganda at all. However, as Augustus could rightfully argue that Rome was a much better place with him in charge, they had limited public support and declining influence of Roman political events. For the vast majority of Romans the achievements of the Augustus regime made its institutional or constitutional arrangements of secondary importance or even irrelevant. The long period of Augustus' personal reign also meant that the regime's propaganda had a long time to influence the Roman people (Holland, 2004, p. 372).

As time went on fewer people could remember the Republican era, yet more of them taught about the anarchy and civil wars that had preceded the Augustus regime and that had subsequently been ended by that regime. Ordinary people passed on the message that the regime had restored and increased the greatness of Rome. That greatness could be easily confirmed by looking at the constructions of the Augustan building programme, such as the Curia Julius, the Forum of Augustus, and the temple of Mars Ultor. The impressive façade of the Augustan building programme could only successfully convey the propaganda messages of the Augustus regime as it achieved real successes, rather than just cosmetic ones (Kean & Frey, 2005 p.28).

The Augustan building programme obviously was intended to convey the message that Augustus was a great man that had been destined to rule Rome and guide the city from troubled times to even greater heights of achievement. Buildings such as the Curia Julius and the temple of Mars Ultor may not have publicly been announced as symbol's of Augustus' exalted political, social and military positions, yet in practice that is what they were conveying to Rome and the rest of the world. The Curia Julius and Mars Ultor had been built to commemorate Julius Caesar who had been declared a God after his death (Claridge, 1998, p. 425). However, in commemorating Julius Caesar they gave glory to his son by adoption, Augustus claimed to be a son of a God giving him a semi-divine status whilst he was still alive. The projects completed as part of the Augustan building programme had plenty of references to

Augustus, such as their titles, statues of him, commemorations of his achievements, alongside details of the regime's military victories (Liberati & Bourbon, 2004, p.42).

The Augustan building programme and other aspects of the regimes propaganda clearly conveyed the message of Augustus' great achievements. The practical aspects of the Augustan building programme and the success of other policies adopted by the regime meant that the majority of people in Rome and in many of the provinces knew that things improved due to the successful policies of the Augustan regime (Holland, 2003, p. 372). For instance, the improved and extended road systems allowed for the improvement of grain supplies from Sicily, Egypt and other African provinces of the empire. Better roads contributed to increasing trade within the empire and allowed the army to reach trouble spots sooner, rather than later (Platner, 1926). To a large extent the message of the regime's achievements rang true, only the poorest and slaves did not directly gain from increased prosperity, stability and peace. Just in case anybody could have forgotten the peace that Rome and the Augustan regime had brought to Rome and the empire, part of the Augustan building programme included a monument to peace. The period of stability led to the use of the phrase ' Pax Romana' and 'Pax Augustus' or the Roman peace and the peace within Rome and its provinces, the maintenance of law and order, both of which was ensured by the strength and the loyalty of the army. The army was responsible for law and order, whilst the expansion of the civil service made administration more effective (Kean & Frey, 2005, p.28).

The main architectural monument to mark the political achievements of Augustus was the Arca Pacis Augustae, which was specifically built to commemorate the peace and glory that Augustus had brought to Rome. Construction of the Arca Pacis Augustae was begun in 13 BC and it was completed four years later. The Senate commissioned the Arca Pacis Augustae to mark Augustus' successful military campaigns in Spain. The monument showed Augustus and his family as well as depicting scenes referring to his political, military and religious roles within the Roman state (Wheeler, 1964, p.9). The main artistic and architectural influences upon this imposing marble arch were in fact Greek. The Arca Pacis Augustae was based on earlier arches found in such cities as Athens, most notably the Alter of Pity. The marble sculpted scenes that made the arch so decorative in appearance and therefore made the political propaganda so much clearer was testament to the skills of the Greek sculptors that sculpted them. Augustus had wished to use Greek sculptors because that they would make the arch look more impressive. The overall effect of the Arca Pacis Augustae was that it met all the propaganda tasks set for it. It displayed the full glory of Rome, it displayed the glory of Augustus whilst portraying the peace and the moral or family values that the Augustan regime represented (Boardman, Griffin, & Murray, 1988, p. 370). As a symbol of Rome's renewal and the rebirth of its greatness the Arca Pacis Augustae was a potent piece of propaganda that conveyed the message that Augustus had restored peace and a sense of destiny to Rome (le Glay, Voison, le Boehec, 2005, p.191).

All the portraits and statues of Augustus that were part of the Augustan building programme and therefore put on public display made Augustus look younger than he actually was. There are hardly any examples of the ageing ruler that were placed in public buildings. The regime did not like to show that Augustus was mortal and would eventually die (Kemp, 2000, p.40). On the other hand Augustus included the construction of his own tomb as part of the Augustan building programme. He regarded his tomb as the most important physical commemoration of his work and his achievements in governing Rome. In propaganda terms it was used in combination with the Res Gestae (Holland, 2003, p. 371). Once completed Augustus' tomb was situated in the Campus Martius and measured a massive 87 metres in diameter, in design it was similar Etruscan tombs, just much bigger. The tomb was intended to allow Augustus' successors to reflect in his glory and authority. Unfortunately for Augustus most of his designated successors had died before him, his ashes were placed in the tomb after theirs (Ramage & Ramage, 1991, p. 84).

The rebuilding of large parts of Rome gave substance to Augustus' claim that he had replaced brick buildings with marble ones. The Augustan building programme gave Romans a city that was definitely more pleasing on their eyes (Platner, 1926, p. 125). The reconstruction of Rome meant that the city looked the part of being the epicentre of the world's largest empire. Nobody could miss the grandness of new Augustan Rome; it would have been virtually impossible not to be impressed by the Curia Julius, the Mars Ultor, or the Apollo Sosiarius. The improved road system meant that more outsiders could also be impressed by the magnificence of Rome. Logically, being impressed by the Augustan building programme entailed being impressed by the regime that was responsible for erecting such imposing buildings. The scale of the Augustan building programme was only achievable due to the financial and administrative reforms that the regime instigated. Although the Egyptian confiscated treasure that Augustus returned with had been substantial, it would not have covered the entire cost of the Augustan building programme (Kean & Frey, 2005, p.28).

Concluding Remarks

Therefore the Augustan building programme was influenced by the aims, policies and strategies pursued by the Augustan regime. Augustus considered the Augustan building programme as being a central part of his strategy for consolidating his power and his positions. Before Augustus the Romans had constructed some fine buildings that showed a strong Greek design influence. Rome had been built in an ad hoc way, population expansion and neglect caused by the civil wars meant that Julius Caesar had already planned a major reconstruction of the city before his death. The belief that Julius Caesar should be commemorated had a catalytic influence on the starting of the building programme, especially after he became deified. Religion, as well as commemoration had a strong influence upon the Augustan building programme. On some projects the desire to commemorate had coincided with religious influences. For instance the completion of the temple of Mars Ultor and the Arca Pacis Augustae. Another theme held another influence on the Mars Ultor, the military and naval victories achieved by Roman forces, with particular reference to the naval victory at Actium, which allowed the subsequent military conquest of Egypt. The Romans often regarded commemoration, religion, and military victories as being closely connected. The veneration of the Gods was considered to be highly important for the success of Rome, particularly to Mars, whose influence upon the city's destiny was believed to be highly influential. There were numerous other temples in Rome that were dedicated to Gods that were imported from the places the Romans had taken over, the Greek Gods such as Apollo had proved to be rather popular. Greek architecture had strong influences upon the Roman buildings with features such as pillars and domes. Greek religion, culture, and literature had been exported into Roman culture. Roman legions may have conquered Greece, yet Greek ideas took deep roots in Roman culture and political thought. In theory, Greek political thought would have reinforced Roman republicanism, however that did prove to be the case in practice.

Concepts about the renovation and renewal of Rome had a strong influence upon the former and scope of the Augustan building programme. Rome needed to have a major overhaul by the time that Augustus gained undisputed power. Not only did the city's buildings need improving but also taxation system, transport, alongside the law and order infrastructure which had to be improved as well. The major constructions of Augustan building programme may have gained the most public attention, yet the improvement of the roads and bridges probably did more to boost trade and prosperity. The desire to build big impressive buildings was a major influence upon the Augustan building programme. Buildings were built to impress Romans and outsiders alike, they were designed to demonstrate the power of Rome in general and the might of the Augustan regime in particular.

Therefore, the propaganda objectives and the public relations messages of the Augustan regime were probably the most prominent influences upon the completion of the Augustan building programme. At the beginning of the Augustan regime Augustus wished to use the Augustan building programme as a means to promote his personal rule and consolidate his position. Whilst Augustus wished to use the Augustan building programme as a means of showing his powerful position to the Roman public, he also wanted to give the impression that his regime was not the replacement for the Roman Republic. Although in actual fact he had by-passed the institutions of the Roman Republic. Augustus used the Augustan building programme in his propaganda efforts to portray himself as the restorer of peace, stability, and prosperity to Rome and the empire. The desire to make Rome a better place was certainly reflected in the achievements of the Augustan building programme, the Mars Ultor, the Forum of Augustus, the Curia Julius alongside the Pantheon were all magnificent symbols of Rome's power, peace and prosperity. Of course not everybody benefited from the policies of the Augustan regime, yet most people were better off and safer than in the last years of the Roman Republic. Officially the Augustan regime did not mark the end of the Roman Republic, yet in practice that is exactly what happened.

In many respects the Augustan building programme was influenced by the Augustan regime's objective of providing favourable publicity for Augustus with the intention of increasing his personal prestige. Increasing the glory of Augustus contradicted the statements that the Roman Republic had not been ended by the creation of the Augustan regime. Propaganda was slanted to convey the message that the great, wise and peace loving Augustus had saved Rome from Republican decadence and civil war, which meant that he was entitled to be given extra positions, powers and honours. As Rome's saviour Augustus was granted special powers for life and argued that he should be able to pass them on to his nominated heir. Augustus was very careful to use the Augustan building programme to increase his prestige, and power, yet he remained astute enough to maintain the pretence that Rome remained a republic. He had resisted the temptation to be named as a king or made a dictator for life to minimise republican opposition, and therefore retain stability throughout the Roman Empire. The adopted title of Augustus Caesar had aided the transformation of Octavianus from being the young great nephew of Julius Caesar fighting to keep his inheritance to becoming the ruler of the world's largest empire. The new title had increased his prestige, yet he held power via the holding of several offices, and the effective use of special powers granted to him by the Senate and the Roman tribunes. Augustus' abilities as a political leader, administrator, and military commander meant his positions, and powers were effectively manipulated to wield supreme power. The complexity of Roman constitutional arrangements was not always a good thing for his successors, yet those arrangements had allowed the Augustan regime to operate effectively. Political motives probably remained the greatest combined influence upon the constructions and projects that formed the Augustan building programme. For Rome and its leader to be great in image as well as in reality, meant that the buildings of the city had to look the part, after the Augustan building programme that could certainly be argued was the case for Rome.

There were other non-political influences upon the design and completion of the Augustan building programme. These influences included cultural influences such as the strong sense of militarism that could be detected in Roman society. Other influences upon the Augustan building programme were pragmatic considerations, such as the availability of building materials, or preferred design features such as domes. The relatively advanced construction and engineering techniques of the Romans were a bonus for the Augustan regime when it came to completing its building regime.

Bibliography

Augustus, Res Gestae

Beard M & Crawford M, (2004) Rome in the Late Republic 2nd edition, Duckworth, London

Boardman J, Griffin J, & Murray O, (1988) The Roman World, Oxford University Press, Oxford

Castleden R, (2005) Events that changed the world, Time Warner Publishing, New York and London

Claridge A, (1998) Rome, Oxford

Crystal D, (1998) The Cambridge Biographical Encyclopedia, 2nd edition, Cambridge University Press, Cambridge

Davies N, (1996) Europe – a History, Oxford University Press, Oxford

Favro D, (1996) The urban image of Augustan Rome, Cambridge

Galinsky K, (1996) Augustan Culture: An Interpretative Introduction, Princeton

Garnsey & Saller, (1987) The Roman Empire – Economy, Society and Culture, London

Goldsworthy A, (2003) In the name of Rome, the men who won the Roman Empire, Weidenfeld & Nicholson, London

Grant M, (1996) The Roman Emperors – A biographical guide to the rulers of Imperial Rome 31 BC – AD 476, Phoenix Giant, London

Holland T, (2003) Rubicon – the Triumph and the Tragedy of the Roman Republic

Honour H & Fleming J (1999) A World History of Art, Lawrence King Publishing

Horace, Epodes

Kean R M & Frey O, (2005) The Complete Chronicle of the Emperors of Rome, Thalamus Publishing, Ludlow

Kemp M, (2000) The Oxford History of Western Europe, Oxford University Press, Oxford

Le Glay, Voisin, & le Bohec, (2005) A History of Rome 3rd edition, Blackwell Publishing

Liberati A M, & Bourbon F, (2004) Ancient Rome, History of a Civilization that ruled the world, White Star Publishers, Verceli

Neal J, (2004) Architecture – A visual history, Greenwich Editions, London

Ovid - Fasti

Parry, (2005) Engineering the Ancient World, Sutton Publishing, Stroud

Platner S B, (1926) A topographical Dictionary of Rome, Oxford

Ramage N H, & Ramage A, (1991) The Cambridge Illustrated History of Roman Art, Cambridge University Press, Cambridge

Roberts J.M, (1996) A History of Europe, Penguin, London

Rodgers N, (2005) The Roman World, People and Places, Lorenz Books, London

Schnapp A, (1993) The discovery of the Past, British Museum Press, London

Seutonius, the Deified Augustus

Speake, (1994) The Penguin Dictionary of Ancient History, Penguin, London

Virgil, Aeneid

Wheeler M, (1964) Roman art & Architecture, Thames & Hudson, London

Zanker P, (1988) The Power of Images in the Age of Augustus, Ann Arbor

Printed in Great Britain
by Amazon

23691984R00020